Reptile Keeper's Guides

DAY GECKOS

R. D. Bartlett
Patricia Bartlett

BARRON'S

Acknowledgments

When you begin talking to other reptile fanciers about geckos, they quickly divide themselves into two camps—those who think geckos are "fine little lizards" and those who are hopelessly, totally entranced by these intriguing lizards. Although not all of the people listed here are inveterate gecko-philes, they have all provided us with advice or photographic opportunities. We deeply appreciate and acknowledge the assistance of Bill Brant, Ralph Curtis, Scott Hearsey, Rob MacInnes, Sean McKeown, Mike Stuhlman, and Tim Tytle. Sincere thanks are also extended to our editor, Anna Damaskos.

All inquiries should be addressed to:
Barron's Educational Series, Inc.
250 Wireless Boulevard
Hauppauge, NY 11788
http://www.barronseduc.com

Library of Congress Catalog Card No. 2001025445

International Standard Book No. 0-7641-1699-1

Library of Congress Cataloging-in-Publication Data
Bartlett, Richard D., 1938–
  Day geckos / R. D. Bartlett and Patricia Bartlett.
   p. cm. — (Reptile keeper's guide)
  ISBN 0-7641-1669-1
   1. Phelsuma. 2. Geckos as pets. I. Bartlett,
 Patricia Pope, 1949– . II. Title.
SF459.G35 B36 2001
639.3'952—dc21   2001025445

Printed in Hong Kong
9 8 7 6 5 4 3 2 1

Contents

Introduction
2

What Are Day Geckos?
4

Choosing Your Day Gecko
15

Caging
25

Diet
31

Health
33

Breeding
38

Glossary
44

Helpful Information
45

Index
46

Introduction

Sean McKeown has referred to day geckos as "living jewels of the Indian Ocean." One merely has to look into a terrarium setup with a family group of these brilliantly colored creatures, all actively exploring their tank, to understand the comparison.

At one time day geckos were considered rare and delicate. Those that made it to a hobbyist often were plagued with then-mysterious maladies called "rubberleg" or "soft-jaw." Day geckos are no longer thought of in that manner. In fact, species and subspecies that were once thought to be difficult captives and were so uncommonly seen in herpetoculture that only the luckiest (or most dedicated) of hobbyists would have them, are now commonplace. You can easily find many of these former rarities in herp ads, on the World-Wide Web, and at herp expos.

Day geckos diverge from nocturnality, the norm for most members of geckodom, by being diurnally active. The name is traditionally reserved for the many members of the genus *Phelsuma*. This group contains approximately sixty species of geckos that are found primarily on the island continent of Madagascar and its surrounding islets, but also occur in small numbers on the Andaman, Comoro, Seychelles, and a few other Indian Ocean islands. The island of Rodrigues continues to have its own populations of day geckos, but the island was also once home to two very large and now extinct species. These were *P. edwardnewtoni* and *P. gigas*.

The orange dorsal markings of the large-blotched lined day gecko have merged into a large primary blotch followed by several smaller ones.

Madagascar has some twenty species of day geckos, and sixteen of these are endemic to the island. To protect these fragile lizards from exploitation, the island has established export quotas (although these are seemingly continually changing).

Although a few gray and brown species exist, the day geckos are, for the most part, among the most brightly colored of lizards. Most are clad in Kelly green and accented dorsally with a varying amount of bright orange or blue.

The day geckos range in size from the small neon day gecko, *P. klemmeri,* which is adult at a total length of 3 inches, to the very large (12-inch) Standing's day gecko, *P. standingi.* Most of the species, however, are in the 5- to 7-inch size range. All have expanded digital discs, which enable them to climb vertically on glass, and lidless eyes bearing round pupils. Day geckos are omnivorous, consuming insects but pollen, nectar, overripe fruits, and saps and juices as well. Of the roughly sixty species, several are critically imperiled because of continuing habitat degradation.

Sexually mature male day geckos are extremely territorial and will skirmish constantly with others of their sex to establish territorial dominance. If you are hoping to keep more than a single male to a cage, that cage must be very large and contain a number of visual barriers. If still harassed by the dominant male, subordinate males will need to be removed to their own individual terraria. The females are also hierarchical. If you're planning on keeping all your day geckos in a single cage, select those that are the same size and put them in the cage at the same time. Although it is possible to raise several juvenile day geckos in the same enclosure, they will develop hierarchies as they reach sexual maturity, and aggressive behavior may be manifested.

Day geckos usually do best when kept in sexual pairs or trios of one male and two females. Such groupings usually do not argue with each other, so the individual geckos are more visible and seem to breed well.

Day gecko diets were once a great unknown. To truly thrive, captive day geckos require a well-balanced, vitamin- and mineral-enhanced diet consisting of flower nectar (honey and fruit purees are a good substitute) and insects. Adequate, healthy (full-spectrum) lighting is also necessary.

This 30-gallon tall terrarium is home to 6 pairs of assorted small day geckos. Note the plantings and full-spectrum lighting.

What Are Day Geckos?

Day geckos come in three sizes—small, medium, and large, although deciding which are medium and which are small is sometimes an arbitrary decision. Hobbyists understandably most covet those that are either large or brightly colored, or both. With day geckos, fanciers have a lot of choices.

The majority of the species have a ground color of Kelly or bright green, a few are light green, and fewer yet are gray to brown. A number of the species are being captive-bred by American hobbyists, but a great many of the taxa are bred by dedicated European enthusiasts. Let's take a look at a few day gecko species currently available in the American and European pet trade.

Three of the largest species are the Madagascar giant day gecko, the Standing's day gecko, and the Seychelles giant day gecko. All of these are fully grown at a total length of 8 to 9 inches (although occasional males of the Madagascar giant day gecko, *P. madagascariensis grandis*, may rarely exceed exceed 12 inches long).

Of these three species, both the Madagascar giant day gecko and the Seychelles giant day gecko are subspeciated. The four subspecies of the former vary quite distinctly in color, an important fact to know if you are purchasing these geckos sight unseen.

If you like a considerable amount of bright orange and a background of Kelly green, the giant day gecko, *P. m. grandis*, should be your choice. Not only is this race the most contrastingly colored, but it also is consistently the largest as well. The maroon head markings and equally prominent, (usually) well-defined, orange

The Madagascar day gecko, *P. m. madagascariensis*, attains a length of about 8.5 inches.

dorsal markings contrast sharply with the bright green ground color, and some blue, often on the face, may be present. This remains an abundant race that is widely spread in northern Madagascar and on the surrounding islands.

The next most brilliant in color is the Madagascar day gecko, *P. m. madagascariensis.* At 9 1/2 inches, it averages an inch and a half shorter than *grandis.* It ranges widely in eastern Madagascar as well as some of the eastern islands. A maroon ocular stripe is usually present. The orange spots on the dorsal surface of the head are usually only weakly defined. The green of the dorsum can be variable, ranging from light to dark green. The orange spots of the dorsum are often arranged in three weakly defined longitudinal rows, the vertebral row being the best defined. The lateral scales are tuberculate, those of the jowls prominently so.

The remaining two races are less commonly seen in captivity. These are Boehm's and Koch's day geckos. The former is adult at about 8 inches, but

Koch's subspecies of the giant day gecko tend to be less brilliantly green than the other three races.

The blue-tailed day gecko, *P. cepediana,* is variably, but always beautifully, colored.

The prominent banding of this hatchling Boehme's giant day gecko, *P. madagascariensis boehmei*, will fade with growth.

Koch's day gecko may attain 10 inches.

Boehm's giant day gecko, *P. m. boehmi*, is restricted in distribution to the central eastern coast of Madagascar. The largest orange markings are in the forms of dots and dashes on the dorsal

This adult Boehme's giant day gecko is cleaning its brille (the clear scale covering its eye) with its tongue.

surface of the head. A broad ocular stripe is present, beginning above the tympanum and converging on the tip of the snout. Numerous orange dots and short dashes are present over most of the dorsum. The lateral scales are prominent and noticeably tuberculate.

Koch's giant day gecko lacks most of the contrasting orange markings. *P. m. kochi* is found in western and northwestern Madagascar. The scales of the sides and jowls are prominently tuberculate.

Although most herpetocultural efforts have been directed at propagating *P. m. grandis*, the other

three races are also bred extensively. Courtship by the males of all races is aggressive, and spacious cages and multiple visual barriers are necessary to prevent the females from being injured by the larger males.

Egg-laying females orient themselves nearly vertically between the leaves of stiff-leafed plants such as sansevierias, bananas, or in captivity, bromeliads. They lay an egg, hold it in their rear feet until the shell has dried, then place the egg in the axils of the plant. Clutches consist of two eggs. The eggs are nonadhesive and can be easily removed to an incubator.

Brilliantly colored when hatched, Standing's day geckos undergo considerable ontogenetic changes.

This male gold-dust day gecko is so heavily dusted with gold specks that the green is almost obscured.

Standing's day gecko, *P. standingi*, is grayish-green or bluish-green when adult but is strongly banded with russet and blue-gray when hatched. The head and shoulders of the adults can be reticulated with dark pigment. The ontogenetic changes undergone by this foot-long gecko are remarkable. This is a heavy-bodied, very impressive species. Although lacking the brilliance of many of its congeners, Standing's day geckos display a unique and subtle beauty. Standing's day geckos may live for more than fifteen years when properly cared for.

Of the three races of Seychelles giant day gecko, only the nominate race, *P. sundbergi sundbergi*, is seen with any regularity in America. Truthfully, it may be necessary to search hard to find even this 8-inch beauty.

The brilliant Kelly green ground color of the active adult Seychelles giant day gecko may dull noticeably when the lizard is at rest or at night. There is (often) a difficult to discern peppering of tiny orange spots dorsally as well as a fairly well-defined orange canthal bridle. A poorly defined, anteriorly directed, interorbital bridle is usually present. The lips are often a quite bright blue. This gecko is found on the island of

P. l. laticauda has derived its common name of gold-dust day gecko from the liberal peppering of gold spots on the back.

A single large dorsal marking is typical of *P. laticauda angularis*, the northwestern gold-dust day gecko.

The yellow-throated day gecko is captive bred in small numbers.

Praslin as well as surrounding islands and islets of the northeastern Seychelles.

One of the most beautiful of the medium-sized day geckos is also considered one of the more delicate species. This is *P. cepediana*, from Maritius. It is commonly called the blue-tailed day gecko. It is sexually dimorphic, the males being the more brilliant and larger of the sexes. There seems to be considerable altitudinal variation in pattern and marking intensity, those of the highlands being less brilliant than their lowland equivalents.

The males are colored an intense turquoise to almost robin's-egg blue dorsally, often patterned with brilliant orange lateral and dorsolateral striping as well as dorsal spots and stripes. The sides of the face and anterior lateral surfaces are intense green. The tail is brilliant blue. Females are smaller, less brilliantly colored, and less contrastingly patterned. Adult males occasionally near a 6-inch overall length, but 4 1/2 to 5 inches is more typical.

The pretty gold-dust day gecko, *P. laticauda*, attains a length of 5 inches. The common name refers to the liberal peppering of yellow on the nape and

It is from the four large blue-edged black lateral markings that the peacock day gecko has derived its name.

This peacock day gecko, *P. q. quadriocellata*, is very prettily marked.

The flattened, flanged tail of the flat-tailed day gecko, *P. serraticauda*, is diagnostic of the species.

The flat-tailed day gecko is one of the more aggressive taxa.

P. laticauda is a hardy and easily bred species. The eggs are easily incubated and the hatchlings are about 1 1/2 inches in overall length. This species readily consumes both insect prey and gecko formula.

shoulder area. The gold-dust day gecko is usually a brilliant green, but may have a bluish-green tinge on the sides, limbs, and feet. Some specimens may display a yellowish wash on their dorsal surface. A trio of elongated, orange teardrop markings adorn the middorsum. These markings are followed posteriorly by a varying number of smaller orange markings that may be discrete or coalesce into a vaguely reticulate pattern. The tail is quite flattened. This gecko is widely distributed on Madagascar, the Comoros, and the Seychelles, and has been introduced to some of the Hawaiian Islands. The northwestern gold-dust day gecko, *P. l. angularis*, from northwestern Madagascar, is smaller, somewhat less colorful, and has an even more flattened tail. Some authorities consider it a full species. Besides the other dorsal markings an inverted orange chevron is present anterior to the teardrops.

For many people, the peacock day gecko, *P. quadriocellata* ssp., is one of the most beautiful of all lizard species. There are three subspecies found in eastern Madagascar. The leaf-green dorsum is peppered anteriorly with turquoise. A blue chevron often appears on the snout, its apex above the nostrils. The dorsum is variably marked with orange dots and dashes from the shoulders to the anterior tail. The name, *quadriocellata,* translates literally to "four spots" and refers to a turquoise-outlined black spot posterior to each forelimb and a dark marking (usually not actually a spot) anterior to each hind limb.

This is basically an arboreal species that commonly attains a rather robust 4 1/2-inch overall length. Because it is another aggressive species, it may be necessary to separate males from females except for breeding interludes.

Seipp's day gecko was only described in 1987.

The dorsal spots of the nominate form of the lined day gecko, *P. l. lineata* are small and numerous.

The Grand Comoro day gecko, *P. v-nigra comoraegrandensis*, is a small and brilliantly colored taxon.

The eggs of the peacock day gecko are moderately adhesive when freshly laid. Those laid in the hollows of cut bamboo are usually rather well secured; those affixed to yielding leaves are more easily dislodged. The hatchlings are just a little more than 1 inch in length when emerging from the paired eggs. Although preferring high humidity, peacock day geckos are hardy and can be prolific breeders if properly cycled.

The beautiful yellow-throated day gecko, *P. flavigularis*, and the closely allied flat-tailed day gecko, *P. serraticauda*, are two beautiful day geckos that are no longer frequently seen in American herpetoculture. These, and the very pretty Seipp's day gecko, *P. seippi*, are still bred in considerable numbers by German hobbyists. *P. flavigularis* occurs in eastern Madagascar. It is primarily green dorsally, and has orange interstices (the

Difficult to identify, Pasteur's day gecko, *P. v-nigra pasteuri*, is often less precisely patterned than the other races, and may have a blue nape blotch.

The Moheli Island day gecko, *P. v-nigra v-nigra*, is a light but bright green and is profusely spotted dorsally with orange.

As a juvenile, the neon day gecko is remarkably beautiful.

skin between the scales) and orange spots. It has blue surrounding the eyes, orange bars bridging the nose, and a lemon-yellow throat. The tail is somewhat flattened. It is 5 inches in total length. *P. serraticauda* is about an inch longer, has a very flattened tail with flanged edges, but is otherwise very similar in appearance to the yellow-throat. It occurs in many northern areas of eastern Madagascar.

Seipp's day gecko, *P. seippi*, was rather recently described (1987). It is 5 1/2 inches in length. A pretty species, the green ground color is a shade or two less intense than the Kelly green worn by many of its congeners. The green of the dorsum is peppered with orange and there is a well-defined bridle of orange between the eyes. A well-defined maroon chevron extends from the snout to a point well posterior to each eye. It, too, occurs in northeastern Madagascar.

Males of the yellow-throated and flat-tailed day geckos can so dominate a small cage that they will have to be removed from the females except for the purpose of breeding. The paired eggs of both species are adhesive when first laid but are all too easily dislodged and damaged. This is especially so when deposited on the rather yielding leaf of a plant.

Seipp's day gecko is less aggressive than the yellow-throat or the flattail. The female Seipp's day geckos place their paired eggs in terrestrial situations, often beneath pieces of cork bark.

The Comoros Island day gecko, *P. comorensis*, and the four subspecies of *P. v-nigra* have recently become rather readily available in the American pet trade. Both species are about 4 inches long. They all hail from the Comoros Islands. The common names of the various races of the latter are derived from the islands on which they are found or from their patronym. Thus, *P. v. v-nigra* is the Moheli Island day gecko, *P. v. pasteuri* is Pasteur's day gecko, *P. v. anjouanensis* is the Anjouan Island day gecko, and *P. v. comoraegrandensis* is

P. guttata is called the spotted day gecko.

called the Grand Comoro day gecko. The subspecies of *P. v-nigra* are best determined by origin rather than color differences, for the latter are slight, seemingly being determined by the comparative size and abundance of the orange dorsal spots.

P. v-nigra ssp. are pretty, bright green geckos with many tiny (*P. v. v-nigra*) or fewer larger (*P. v. pasteuri*), orange spots on the dorsum. The facial and head bars are often only poorly defined. A blue suffusion may be present on the nape.

P. comorensis is dull green with tiny flecks of orange over most of its back. A suffusion of dull orange may appear posterodorsally and on the nose. There is a reddish and a white lateral stripe on each side. The eggs of these two species have adhesive shells.

The lined day gecko, *P. lineata* ssp., is a rather flattened species which, although recorded up to nearly 5 inches in length, is more often seen at a length of slightly less than 4 inches. There are at least five subspecies that, collectively,

Often a mottled gray in color, some muted day geckos, *P. mutabilis*, have attractive blue tails.

P. dubia is appropriately called the dull day gecko.

range over much of the northern half of the island of Madagascar. The subspecies of this gecko vary in availability, but one or the other remains rather consistently available and is comparatively inexpensive.

The male of the lined day gecko is a more intense green, and larger than the female. The dorsum may be decorated with numerous isolated red markings, or the markings may coalesce into a sizable orange blotch. There is a reddish lateral stripe that is often bordered with maroon, then white, ventrally.

Captive lined day geckos like to place their eggs in cavities. The hollow ends of suitably sized vertical bamboo shoots are particularly favored. The egg is weakly adherent.

The neon day gecko, *P. klemmeri,* was described in 1990. Although tiny, its beauty is striking. The head is chartreuse or lime-green. The dorsum is turquoise anteriorly and olive-tan posteriorly. The tail is turquoise, brightest distally. The limbs are olive-tan obscurely peppered with lighter pigment. A broad black lateral line is present from tympanum to groin. This is bordered beneath by the white of the venter. The surface of the head is peppered with tiny black speckles. There are two blue dots, one in the black post tympanal stripe and one

immediately anterior to the shoulder, on each side. This tiny, flattened day gecko attains a 3-inch overall length.

Klemmeri dwells in coastal northwestern Madagascar where, ostensibly, it lives on large, rough-barked trees, retreating into bark crevices and hollows when threatened. The flattened conformation of klemmeri dictates that it be maintained in absolutely escape-proof terraria.

In the terrarium this species lays its eggs in leaf sheaths of bamboo as

This male neon day gecko inspects his realm.

When content, male ornate day geckos, *P. o. ornata*, are very brightly colored.

well as inside the hollows of bamboo stems. They will adhere to such surfaces but are easily dislodged.

P. guttata is known as the spotted day gecko. Although it occasionally attains a length of nearly 5 inches, most specimens are somewhat less than 4 inches in overall length. This lizard has a bluish-green or light green ground color that is strongly and variably spotted with both brick-red and dark spots. A dark line extends from the snout through the eye and terminates above the tympanum (external eardrum), and the top of the head is patterned with stripes rather than spots. The nonadhesive eggs of this gecko may be easily moved to an incubator.

The spotted day gecko is a species of the scrub and introduced banana trees in an area of eastern Madagascar now stripped of its primary forests.

Two day geckos of dull coloration include the moderately sized drab day gecko, *P. mutabilis*, and the dull day gecko, *P. dubia*. Both are brown to gray in coloration and are found on the west coast of Madagascar. *P. dubia* also occurs in the Comoros Islands, and in isolated colonies in coastal Africa. Both species inhabit hot, semi-arid regions. Both may occasionally be found on the ground. Both species are egg gluers.

A third dull-colored species is the Round Island day gecko, *P. guentheri*. It is an endangered species that often attains 10 inches in total length. It is seen only in zoos. *P. guentheri* has a vertically elliptical pupil, indicating a more nocturnal lifestyle than that of most of its congenerics.

Finally, we'll make mention of the small (4-inch) ornate day gecko, *P. ornata* ssp. It is the nominate species, *P. o. ornata*, indigenous to Mauritius, that is most often seen in America. This lizard has a blue-green dorsum bearing rows of large orange spots, a red-orange head with a broad blue bar on the snout, and a brown nape with a white stripe on either side. It is only sporadically available, but more intensive captive-breeding programs that are now being developed should assure a more steady supply. This remarkably beautiful lizard may either descend to the ground to place its pair of eggs beneath a rock or bark shards, or place them behind the loose bark of a standing tree.

Many other day geckos are occasionally available in the United States. You may find many advertised on the Web, in the classified sections of reptile magazines, or on the price lists of dealers. Almost all are easily kept, most are easily bred, and all are deserving of the title "a living jewel."

Choosing Your Day Gecko

Although many reptiles and amphibians are chosen by hobbyists because of the ease with which they can be handled or the fact that one species may be more easily fed or is more brightly colored than another, this is not the case at all with day geckos. None of the species is easily handled, all of them eat pretty much the same food, all require almost identical cages (large species do require bigger cages than small species), and about 95 percent of the day gecko species are very brightly colored. Perhaps food availability should enter into your choice of the day gecko species chosen also. The honey-fruit mixture needed by these geckos is suitable for species of all sizes, but if the only insects readily available to you are adult crickets or adult mealworms, you should not buy a small type of day gecko nor should you purchase a baby of a large species.

As you can see here, the greatest variables that you have to work with in selecting a species of day gecko are the lizard's size, the quantity you wish to keep, food availability, and cage size. The large species, such as the Madagascar and the Seychelles giant, and the Standing's day geckos, require relatively large cages (but they can also eat large insects). For a pair or a trio (one male and two females) of any of these species, we suggest a vertically oriented terrarium of at least 50-gallon capacity, and we actually prefer 75-gallon terraria or large cages. Although you certainly can keep small species in large cages, doing the opposite (keeping large species in small cages) is not an option.

Thus, the size of your caging and the availability of food should play the primary roles in determining the species of day gecko you choose. The former should also determine the number of geckos housed in each enclosure and how complex the interior arrangements of each cage will be. For a longer discussion of this, we refer you to the chapter on caging (pages 25–30). Do remember, though, that day geckos are arboreal lizards, and

On the alert, this adult Madagascar giant day gecko is ready to jump to a new position.

that their needs will be best served if they are housed in vertically oriented terraria. Thus, when considering the space in which to place your terrarium, you will not have to allocate the full 48 by 18 inches usually needed for a conventionally oriented 75-gallon tank. Rather, by placing the tank vertically, you will need only the horizontal space for a small end. Remember, whether horizontal or vertical, the terrarium must be tightly covered.

Handling Your Day Gecko

Day geckos are alert and fast. They become even more so at the slightest hint of danger. Even long-term captives usually equate an approaching hand with grave danger. The easiest and most concise instruction we can offer regarding handling day geckos is the single word *don't*. These beautiful lizards are lizards to observe, appreciate, and learn from. They are not lizards that can be handled.

When it does become necessary to handle your day geckos, do so firmly but gently. Allowing them to squirm in your grasp will only accentuate the possibility of their very delicate skin being torn. Most tears will heal over quickly, and even considerable scars will virtually disappear after a lizard sheds its skin several times, but at the very least, the encounter is stressful to the lizard. There is also the possibility that if you grasp the day gecko incorrectly, its tail will be broken. It may take only a mere bump from you to cause the gecko to autotomize the tail.

There are ways to move your day geckos other than grasping them by hand. If you are moving them from a small to a larger cage, you can simply place the former in the latter and remove the top or open the door of the smaller one. Then secure the larger one and let the geckos move out at their own speed. A second way is to place a large cup upside down over the gecko. You can then slide a piece of rigid plastic or cardboard between the ground and the cup opening and move the lizard without ever actually touching it.

When they feel secure, day geckos are not at all secretive. Depending on

This Comoro day gecko demonstrates that many of these lizards are as at ease inverted as right-side-up.

The toepads allow day geckos to easily cling to smooth, inverted surfaces. This is a southwestern day gecko, *P. leiogaster*.

the species, some will prefer to sit in a head-down position on a vertical log, on the terrarium glass, or on a stalk of bamboo. Others situate themselves horizontally on elevated limbs. Some species may perch on a flat leaf if this is available to them.

The trick, if it can be called this, to keeping day geckos visible in the terrarium is to keep them feeling comfortable and unthreatened.

Of course, when first placed in a terrarium, a day gecko will immediately seclude itself, and may remain hidden for hours or days until it feels secure in its new surroundings. Once it feels at home, the lizard will begin emerging from its sanctuary, sometimes slowly, sometimes quickly, and will choose a basking perch to which it will return time and again. Although the gecko is now used to its quarters, it still may sidle out of sight as you approach, but will eventually become fully used to its surroundings and to motions outside of the cage.

Although some hobbyists feed their day geckos only every second day, we keep fruit-honey mixture available to ours at all times, and offer them gut-loaded crickets every other day. Other insects (waxworms, butterworms, flightless houseflies) are periodically offered. The insects are simply dropped into the gecko's

Day geckos, like this adult Standing's day gecko, often "squirrel" around a limb, keeping a barrier between them and a person approaching.

terrarium. The fruit-honey mixture is fed fresh daily and is offered in shallow dishes propped on the cool end of the elevated basking limb.

The habitats and populations of many species of day geckos are diminishing, so if you have a choice between a wild-collected or a captive-bred-and-hatched specimen, choose the latter.

This male ornate day gecko is drinking the vitamin-mineral enhanced fruit-honey mixture that is continually provided.

The Day Geckos of Today and Yesteryear

Common name	Scientific name	Average total length
Extinct or status unknown:		
Rodrigues Island day gecko	P. edwardnewtoni (extinct)	8″
Rodrigues Island giant day gecko	P. gigas (extinct)	20–25″
Three-lined day gecko	P. trilineata	4″
(The three-lined day gecko's status is unknown. It has not seen since the mid-1800s. Known from only a single specimen.)		
Lined day gecko	P. minuthi	3.5″
(The lined gecko's status is unknown. It was described in 1980 but is known only from the type specimen. It is in the P. lineata complex.)		
Extant:		
Egg gluers		
Andaman Islands day gecko	P. andamanensis	5.25″
(natural and disturbed xeric habitats)		
Barbour's day gecko	P. barbouri	4.75″
(terrestrial and saxicolous in low-humidity grassy regions)		
Reunion and Agalega day geckos	P. borbonica ssp.	5.5″
(natural and disturbed xeric habitats)		
Blue-tailed day gecko	P. cepediana	5.25″
(natural and disturbed, high-humidity habitats)		
Comoro Island day gecko	P. comorensis	4.5″
(natural and disturbed habitats with variable humidity)		
Dull day gecko	P. dubia	5″
(natural and disturbed, variably humid, lowland habitats)		
Round Island day gecko	P. guentheri	8–9.5″
(humid palm habitats)		
Mauritius forest day geckos		
(both races)	P. guimbeaui	4–6.5″
(high humidity forested and disturbed habitats)		
Southern lined day gecko (all races)	P. leiogaster	3.75″
(low vegetation in disturbed xeric habitats)		
Modest day gecko	P. modesta	3″
(arid regions)		
Pemba Island day gecko	P. parkeri	3.5″
(coastal and interior areas of variable humidity)		
V-nigra day geckos (all races)	P. v-nigra ssp.	4″
(variable humidity, variable habitats)		
Weakly adhesive eggs		
Northwestern day gecko	P. beufotakensis	4.25″
(natural and disturbed habitats with varying humidity)		
Boettger's day gecko	P. breviceps	3.25″
(disturbed arid habitats)		
Two-spotted peacock day gecko	P. (quadriocellata) bimaculata	4.75″
(rain forest and riparian habitats)		

Common name	Scientific name	Average total length
Yellow-throated day gecko	*P. flavigularis*	5″
(natural and disturbed habitats with varying humidity)		
Neon day gecko	*P. klemmeri*	3″
(rain forest habitats)		
Northern lined day gecko (all races)	*P. lineata* ssp.	4–5.25″
(high-humidity habitats)		
Black-lined day gecko	*P. nigristriata*	4.25″
(disturbed xeric and high-humidity habitats)		
Ornate day gecko (both races)	*P. ornata* ssp.	4.5″
(adaptable; trees, rocks, shrubs in areas of varying humidity		
Dwarf day geckos (both races)	*P. pusilla* ssp.	2.75″
(amongst succulents in high-humidity habitats)		
Peacock day geckos (all races)	*P. quadriocellata* ssp.	4.5″
(disturbed and natural areas with varying humidity)		
Merten's day gecko	*P. robertmertensi*	4.25″
(disturbed habitats with variable humidity)		
Flat-tailed day gecko	*P. serraticauda*	4.75–5.5″
(disturbed habitats with variable humidty)		

Nonadhesive eggs

Abbott's day geckos (both races)	*P. abbotti* ssp.	4–5″
(natural and disturbed xeric habitats)		
Seychelles day geckos (both races)	*P. astriata* ssp.	5″
(natural and disturbed xeric habitats)		
Spotted day gecko	*P. guttata*	4″
(high-humidity riparian and forest habitats)		
Gold-dust day geckos (both races)	*P. laticauda* ssp.	4.25″
(very adaptable; natural and disturbed habitats of many types)		
Madagascar giant day geckos (all races)	*P. madagascariensis* ssp.	7–11″
(forest edges and rain forest, also humid disturbed habitats)		
Drab day gecko	*P. mutabilis*	4″
(xeric habitats)		
Seipp's day gecko	*P. seippi*	5.5″
(humid forested areas)		
Standing's day gecko	*P. standingi*	9–10″
(natural and disturbed xeric habitats)		
Seychelles giant day gecko	*P. sundbergi* ssp.	6–9″
(very arboreal; natural and disturbed xeric habitats)		

The distal half of this large-blotched lined day gecko, *P. lineata bifasciata*, has been regenerated. Note the difference in scalation.

Not only are they apt to be better adjusted at the time of purchase, but also your purchase of captive-bred specimens is a positive statement for herpetoculture and a positive step for conservation.

Obtaining Your Day Gecko

The day gecko you select should be stocky, alert, active, have bright coloration, have all of its fingers and toes, not have open wounds, and not have sunken eyes. Whether you select one with a broken or regenerated tail will be largely up to you; neither of the latter is particularly serious, but keep in mind that regenerated tails are never as attractive as the gecko's original tail. Do not select an obviously undernourished gecko, or one with loose stools or with feces smeared at the anal opening. If the gecko you select has been collected from the wild, you may wish to have fecal analysis done by a veterinarian to determine gut-parasite type and load. Do not choose

a gecko that seems thin but has stocky hind limbs.

Many of the day geckos in the pet trade are still wild-collected, but an ever-increasing number are captive-bred. This increase in captive-bred specimens speaks well for not only the hardiness and adaptability of the day geckos, but also for the ever-increasing knowledge and diligence of hobbyists and commercial reptile breeders.

Day geckos can be obtained in any of several ways. Some species may be available at neighborhood pet stores and others from specialty dealers. Many species can be found at captive breeder expos, are sold by the breeders themselves, or are advertised on the Web or in the classified section of reptile magazines. Let's explore some of these avenues of acquisition.

It is probable that by now, you have chosen the kind of day gecko you want from the many species and subspecies available, and have caging readied. For large species such as the Seychelles giant day gecko and the Madagascar giant day gecko, the caging will necessarily be large, a minimum of a 50-gallon tank size. For smaller species such as the Comoro day gecko and the neon day gecko, caging can be more modest, along the lines of a vertical 15-gallon tank.

We advocate purchasing your geckos at local pet stores when possible, for there you can see the animals, discuss them freely with store personnel, personally assess the lizards' health, and watch them feed and interact.

This Comoro day gecko is jumping from a leaf to the glass side of its terrarium.

The Reunion day gecko, *P. ornata inexpectata*, is not often seen in captivity.

There may be some questions that your local pet shop is unable to answer. Among these will be the origin of a given wild-collected specimen, or the history and genetics of a specific day gecko. In most cases the history of a gecko becomes irretrievably lost once the animal enters the commercial pet trade. The single exception to this will be the records available from breeders, should you decide to buy direct.

In many areas of the world, herp expos are now held on a regular basis. In the United States they are held in many of our larger cities, some annually, some quarterly, and some monthly. The expos are usually well advertised in the various reptile magazines and on a number of web sites.

An expo is merely a gathering of dealers and breeders all under one roof. Expos vary in size from the 450-plus tables of the National Reptile Breeders' Expo, which is held in Florida every August, to some that are much smaller but quite comprehensive. Not only are day geckos well represented at most of these shows, but support equipment—terraria and cage furniture and the like—is also available.

Breeders are a reliable source for obtaining your day geckos. Breeders may produce only a few clutches of a species or subspecies, or may produce hundreds of hatchlings of numerous taxa. With each passing year, more and more day gecko breeders are present at the various herp expos. Other breeders may advertise in the classified or pictorial ads sections in specialty reptile and amphibian magazines (see the Helpful Information section, page 45). Breeders usually offer parasite-free, well-acclimated specimens and accurate information. Most keep records of genetics, lineage, fecundity, health, or quirks of the species with which they work, and especially of the specimens in their breeding programs.

Reptile dealers have existed at least since the 1940s. Besides often breeding fair numbers of the reptiles

Methods of Shipping

There are options available for shipping lizards that are not available for shipping snakes or turtles. Some are:

Express mail (U.S.P.S.) This is usually a door-to-door pre-paid service, for which your shipper will require payment in advance. The cost is $15 to $25.

Air freight is airport to airport—depending on the airline used, either two or three levels of service are available. Regular, space available freight, costs about $35. Air Express, guaranteed flights, with freight charges collect, about $70. Special Handling, guarantees flights, charges, but must have freight prepaid, costs about $55.)

Other options: Occasionally shipping companies such as Airborne or FedEx will accept lizards (this is the local manager's prerogative). Charges are prepaid, and vary between $15 and $40 for this door-to-door service.

It is usually necessary for someone to be at home to sign for the package on any of the door-to-door services.

Payment: Increasingly, payment requested by shippers is for both the animal(s) and their shipping. Unless the shipper knows you well, you will have to pay in advance (including boxing charges if any) before the animals will be shipped to you. This usually means a money order, cashier's check, a credit card, or wire transfer of funds. Many shippers will accept personal checks but will not ship until the check has cleared their bank (usually a week or so after deposit).

An alternate method of payment is C.O.D. However, because of a hefty C.O.D. surcharge, this can be expensive and is often inconvenient.

To ship, your supplier will need your full name, address, and day and night telephone numbers. Agree on a shipping date. If you elect to use airport-to-airport service, specify which destination airport you wish to use.

Shipping by any service on weekends, holidays, or during very hot or very cold weather may be difficult and should be discouraged. If applicable, pick your shipment up as quickly after its arrival as possible. This is especially important in bad weather. Learn the hours of your cargo office and whether the shipment can be picked up at the ticket counter if it arrives after the cargo office has closed.

You will have to pay for your shipment (including all COD charges and fees) before you can inspect it. Once you are given your shipment, open it before leaving the cargo facility.

Unless otherwise specified, reliable shippers guarantee live delivery. However, to verify the existence of a problem, both shippers and airlines will require a "discrepancy" or "damage" report made out, signed, and dated by airline personnel. In the very rare case when a problem has occurred, insist on filling out and filing a claim form and contact your shipper immediately for instructions.

Ideally, after the first time, you will no longer find the shipping of specimens intimidating. Understanding the system will open wide new doors of acquisition.

Abbott's day gecko, *P. abbotti*, is a small species from the Aldabra Islands that is only occasionally available to hobbyists.

they offer, specialty dealers deal directly with other breeders around the world and may even be direct importers of wild-collected species not yet being captive-bred. Many such dealers both buy and sell reptiles and amphibians at herp expos.

Within the last few years the World-Wide Web has become an important source of information. By instructing your search engine to seek "day geckos" or a specific kind of day gecko you should learn of several hundred breeders, many of whom have excellent photos on their web site.

Herpetological clubs also exist in many cities. You can learn about them by asking at pet stores, museums, college biology departments, or some high schools. At these meetings, if queried, fellow enthusiasts may be able to offer comments about some reptile dealers.

Mail Order Purchase and Shipping

Even today, with herp expos and expanded neighborhood pet stores

now the norm, the day gecko in which you are interested may not be locally available. If this is the case, mail order may be the answer.

First you must find the gecko; then you must contact the advertiser. From the advertiser you should learn about the gecko's feeding habits, age, and other pertinent information.

The shipping of reptiles is not at all the insurmountable barrier that many hobbyists initially think it to be. But it can be expensive. The chances are excellent that the supplier that you have chosen to use is quite familiar with shipping and will be delighted to assist you in any way possible.

Among the things on which you and your shipper will have to agree is the method of payment and the method and date of shipping. The shipping is most safely accomplished when outdoor temperatures are moderate.

Lizards may be shipped in a number of ways. Discuss the pros and cons of each with your shipper. Today there is a growing tendency to use the door-to-door services of carriers such as U.S. Postal Service, UPS, and Federal Express. These are less expensive and often faster than traditional airport-to-airport airline service.

When seen against a piece of newsprint, the tiny size of a hatchling peacock day gecko becomes apparent.

Caging

Because most are brilliantly colored and easily kept, day geckos continue to be popular with hobbyists. These beautiful lizards can be kept in intricate terraria, simple terraria, large wood and wire cages, or even suitably appointed greenhouses.

The size of the adult of the day gecko in which you are interested and the number that you hope to keep should dictate the capacity of the indoor terrarium needed. Day geckos do not tolerate crowding well. For a pair or trio of small to moderately sized geckos, a 15-gallon "tall" tank will provide sufficient space. For a pair or trio of the large species, we suggest nothing smaller than a 30-gallon tall terrarium, and prefer a 50- to 80-gallon size. If constrained too tightly, day geckos may survive but won't thrive and there will be an unnatural amount of squabbling in a group. Because they are persistently arboreal, day geckos do best in a tall (vertically oriented) terrarium.

A Simple Terrarium for Day Geckos

At a total length of 10 to 12 inches, Standing's day gecko is one of the largest species. A trio, adult when

received, lived amicably in a well-lit 65-gallon hexagonal terrarium in the corner of our living room for more than thirteen years. Illumination was provided by both a fluorescent fixture fitted with a full-spectrum bulb and an incandescent "plant-grow" floodlight. This latter provided warmth as well as illumination. Cage furniture included a large, vertically oriented hollow log, a few cross branches of bamboo, a wildly clambering *Epipremnum aureum* (pothos or variegated philodendron), and a feeding platform. The geckos'

Terraria for the smaller day geckos can be beautifully decorated with small flowering orchids (such as these *Dendrobium* cultivars) and foliage plants.

daily container of vitamin-enhanced fruit-honey mixture was placed on the feeding shelf. During daily mistings, the lizards drank droplets of water from the plant leaves. The substrate, merely four inches of sterilized potting soil, never stagnated, and was changed only once in the thirteen years the terrarium was active. The Standing's geckos dwelt in apparently celibate harmony in this setup for the first five years of their captive life, then began breeding. For the last eight years of their lives, the two females produced a combined total of ten to twelve eggs annually. The eggs were laid on the substrate inside the almost upright hollow log and were gathered and moved to an incubator preset for 84°F. Following about eighty-five days of incubation, hatchlings—remarkably beautiful hatchlings—emerged.

A terrarium of standard shape would suffice equally well. You need to realize that all day geckos are talented escape artists. Their terrarium, whatever its shape, must be tightly and totally covered. If your terrarium is oriented in a standard manner and is of a standard shape, covering it is a simple matter. Clip-on screen or wire mesh tops with either molded plastic or galvanized frames are readily available at many pet stores. Tightly covering your terrarium if it is of an odd shape (hexagonal tanks can be difficult to find covers for) or oriented vertically is more problematic.

A metal framed wire top can be used for a vertically oriented terrarium, providing the end on which the tank rests is lifted at least one-half inch above the stand on which it sits. This can be accomplished by placing the tank atop strategically placed 1 by 2 boards.

However, reptile tanks with built-in sliding screen tops are now readily available in many pet stores. These screen tops slide open and closed on molded plastic frames that are permanently affixed to the terrarium. The tops close tightly and are lockable. We consider these terraria an excellent choice for housing day geckos.

If you use a heat lamp, do not put the bulb against the glass of the tank, or the glass will break. We put the bulbs in a metal round reflector and hold the unit about an inch above the glass by affixing alligator clips around the edge of the reflector.

Suggestions For a Movable Outside Day Gecko Cage

Day geckos are heliothermic lizards that bask extensively. Whenever possible, we have provided our lizards access to natural, unfiltered sunshine.

A pair of peacock day geckos bask in the glow and warmth of their full-spectrum light.

Because our breeding facility was in sunny and almost perpetually hot southwest Florida, many of our day geckos were maintained and bred in large outside cages of wood and wire construction. Large casters were attached to the bottom to facilitate cage movement. This allowed us to move the cages with the seasons, spreading them out beneath the shade trees for the spring, summer, and autumn, and bringing them closely together to make the most efficient use of extra heat (when needed) during the winter months. The cages had a bottom and top of 3/4-inch exterior plywood, and were framed with pressure-treated 2 by 2s. A 1/8-inch mesh hardware cloth was chosen for the wire, because this prevents the escape of all but the smallest crickets.

The outside dimensions of the cage, including the casters, are 72 inches high by 48 inches long by 32 inches wide. This allowed the cages to be rolled inside through sliding patio doors if it became really cold for an extended period. The dimensions of the hinged, front-opening door were 24 inches wide by 48 inches high. The wire is stapled to the frame using stainless 3/8-inch-long staples from a standard, hand-powered staple gun. Those staples that don't seat tightly are tapped in with a hammer. Cage furniture includes a potted ficus tree, a number of diagonal and horizontal branches (all 2 to 3 inches in diameter), and hanging pots of vining philodendrons. Fifty pounds of play sand is spread around the bottom of the cage. Although some washes through the wire with each rainstorm or cage cleaning, the sand lasts for several weeks before needing replacing. To thoroughly clean the cage, the lizards are removed, and the uprights, top, and bottom are scrubbed with a dilute bleach solution (1:10, bleach:water). Then the whole cage is hosed thoroughly with a garden hose. New sand is then provided. During the winter months the cages are covered with 4 mil plastic sheeting. This is stapled firmly in place over three sides and the top. The top sheet of plastic is fitted around an above-cage heat lamp. The

This pair of gold-dust day geckos choose the upper glass of their terrarium as a resting site.

Day geckos drink the water misted onto their terrarium sides and plantings. This is a gold-dust day gecko.

This adult Standing's day gecko has chosen a cork bark tube for its resting spot.

front of the cage is covered with a separate sheet of plastic that is stapled only at the top to allow it to be rolled up when the weather is sufficiently warm.

This arrangement works well until outside temperatures drop into the very low 40s; if it is colder than that, the cages must be rolled indoors.

Some Terrarium Basics

Day geckos are persistently arboreal. Although they will often position themselves head downward on vertical trunks, we suggest that the perches in terrariums and cages be more diagonally or horizontally oriented. Illuminate and warm at least one of the horizontal perches (preferably two) from above to provide a suitable area for thermoregulation. Sections of bamboo are ideal perch material. Tank length sections can be held in place by a dollop of latex aquarium sealant on each end. Day geckos of both sexes can be territorial, but the females are invariably less agonistic than two males. Unless you have a

very large terrarium or cage, we suggest that you never keep more than a single male per cage, and that you watch your females carefully to ascertain that they are compatible. If you are keeping more than a single day gecko per terrarium, provide numerous visual barriers. Barriers can be created by crisscrossing perches and smaller sections of bamboo, providing hollow tubes of cork bark in which the geckos can hide, or by winding the stems of leafy vining plants around the perches. Since the dominant specimen in any group will claim the most prominent and satisfactory basking spot, it is important to provide at least two additional areas conducive to the geckos' thermoregulation. Day geckos prefer to drink by lapping pendulous droplets of water from freshly misted plant leaves or bamboo sections. Unless the water surface is roiled with the bubbles from an aquarium air stone (driven by a small vibrator pump), many day geckos will steadfastly refuse to drink from a water dish. Mist the leaves of your plants with tepid water daily. Be certain that your terrarium plants have not been freshly sprayed with insecticides or

A Koch's giant day gecko, *P. madagascariensis kochi*, in profile.

These toepads provide amazing adroitness for climbing day geckos.

These vary from simple, self-standing, fully constructed types available from dealers in storage sheds, through myriad do-it-yourself kits, to elaborate and decorative commercial kinds

liquid fertilizers. Grow commercially procured plants for a couple of weeks outside of the terrarium to allow systemic additives a chance to dissipate. To grow in a terrarium, most plants (even forest plants) will need strong lighting. Two of the most tolerant are the vining aroid *Epipremnum aureum* (pothos) and *Sansevieria hahni* (a small rosette-shaped, sturdy-leafed succulent). Incandescent fixtures using a commercial plant-grow floodlight bulb are ideal. These bulbs will provide warmth for your geckos as well as the necessary illumination for the plants. In addition, a fluorescent full-spectrum bulb should be used. This will provide small amounts of UV-A and UV-B rays for your geckos. These UV rays assist reptiles in properly metabolizing vitamins and minerals and in promoting natural behavior by the lizards.

Greenhouses

Greenhouses of many styles, constructed from several types of materials, are readily available today.

that, unless you are very "handy," are best left to a professional contractor. Greenhouses are becoming ever more popular and can be ideal homes for day geckos, at least during the summer months. Since these little lizards often cling to the glass, the frosty glass panes of winter can cause the loss of toes, or feet, or even the death of the day gecko. Greenhouses with double glazing are better, safer, and far more economical (after the initial purchase price) than single-glazed structures. Greenhouses are usually considered permanent structures, and a building permit is required to legally install one.

Since day geckos are talented escape artists, absolute security is essential. Additionally, heating and

A portrait of a prettily marked peacock day gecko.

This female ornate day gecko hunts insects and pollen in her orchids.

When approached with imagination and forethought the interior of even a small greenhouse can become the focal point of your home and a wonderful home for your geckos.

The Role of UV Lighting

It is now known that the proper metabolizing of calcium by reptiles and amphibians is dependent on the presence of vitamin D3. In nature, the formation (synthesizing) of D3 by heliothermic (sun-basking) lizards is accomplished by the absorption of the ultraviolet wavelength UV-B. Additionally, the wavelength UV-A promotes natural behavior by herps.

cooling units must be entirely screened from the inside to prevent injury to the inhabitants. It is important to secure even those fixtures well above ground level. The base of the greenhouse must be flush against a concrete slab, affixed to a concrete or brick (stem) wall, or be sunk a foot or more below the surface of the ground. This will preclude easy access by outside predators and escape by the creatures with which you are working.

Greenhouses typically exemplify the adage that the grass is always greener elsewhere, and can bring a few square feet of the tropics to even the snowbelt, or the desert to the verdant east. It is important to provide the appropriate plantings, watering, heating, and lighting systems, and cage furniture. The possibility and feasibility of providing a small pond and waterfall, often much wanted accouterments, should be well thought out at the outset. Well-planned ponds and waterfalls can be wonderful and feasible additions to a rain forest theme that would be impossible to construct in any other setting.

Without sufficient D3, calcium will be poorly metabolized by your day gecko. There are three ways of providing the necessary vitamins and minerals for your geckos. First, you can give both as dietary additives. Second, you can install a full-spectrum, UV-producing bulb above the basking perch of your gecko. Third, you can provide access to unfiltered natural sunlight, at least during the summer months. We choose to use all three approaches with our day geckos.

However, it must be mentioned that there can be too much of a good thing also. UV-B actually stimulates the synthesizing of D3, so when a high-quality UV-B emitting bulb or natural sunlight is provided, the D3 calcium supplements should be correspondingly reduced. Sadly, there is no formula for determining the amount or frequency with which supplements should be provided. We can only ask that care be utilized.

Diet

As mentioned earlier, day geckos have complex (but, fortunately, rather easily duplicated) diets. They not only consume insects, but also seek out nectars, pollens, exudates from over-ripe fruits and the fruits themselves, and plant saps.

The fondness of day geckos for sweet fruit and flower products offers you a simple way of administering the necessary vitamin and mineral supplements as well. Without these latter, especially vitamin D3 and calcium, day geckos are quite apt to develop a metabolic bone disorder (once simply called "decalcification" or "rubber bone disease"). Female geckos that are utilizing calcium to form shells for their developing eggs and rapidly growing young will be affected more quickly than adult males or nonovulating females. Ideally, the ratio of calcium to phosphorus should be two to one. A lack of D3 (which enhances calcium metabolism) can create skeletal demineralization and deformities. Conversely, an excess of vitamin D3 can allow over-metabolizing of calcium, and resulting visceral gout. The prudent use of vitamin/mineral supplements is necessary even with full-spectrum lighting, but can be greatly reduced if the geckos are kept outside and allowed access to natural, unfiltered sunlight.

Besides the vitamin enhanced fruit mixture, day geckos eat a variety of insects. The size of the insects necessarily varies with the size of the geckos being fed. The 3-inch-long neon day geckos require fruit fly-sized (or smaller) crickets; the foot-long Standing's and giant day geckos relish larger insects.

You can control the quality of the food insects you offer your day geckos. A poorly fed insect offers little but bulk as a food item. In contrast, a food insect that has fed on a variety of

How to Make Fruit-honey Mixture for Your Day Geckos

Mix
1/3 jar of pureed papaya, apricot, or mixed fruit baby food
1 tablespoon of honey
1/3 eyedropper of Avitron liquid bird vitamins
1/2 teaspoon of Osteoform or Reptivite powdered vitamins
Add enough water to make this mixture a soupy consistency.
A half tablespoon of bee pollen can be added if available.

Feed as needed in elevated dishes.
Refrigerate leftovers, but discard and remake after one week.
Replace the mixture in the cage daily.

Barbour's day gecko is a small, brightly colored blue-tailed species.

nutritious foods, particularly just before being offered to your insectivorous lizards, is a nutritional bonus package.

Foods to offer your feed insects include calcium, vitamin D3, fresh fruit, grated carrots, squash, broccoli, fresh alfalfa and/or bean sprouts, honey, and vitamin/mineral-enhanced (chick) laying mash. A commercially prepared cricket gut-loading diet is now available. (It can be used for mealworms and king mealworms, too.)

Food insects that are commercially available include crickets, mealworms, giant mealworms, waxworms, fruitflies, silkworms, and trevoworms (butterworms). If you need large numbers, get dealers' names and phone numbers from the classifieds in reptile magazines or check the Web. The latter often provides instant online ordering opportunities as well. If you need only small numbers of feed insects, your local pet or feed store may be your most economical source.

Day geckos enter the cups of baby crickets to eat.

Health

If they are fed and housed properly, day geckos are trouble-free, long-lived lizards, but medical problems requiring the assessment and intervention of a veterinarian may arise occasionally. Not all veterinarians are comfortable treating reptiles, nor are all qualified to do so. We suggest that you find a suitable veterinarian before the need for one actually arises. Check the Yellow Pages of your local phone book, ask the veterinarian who treats your dog or cat for a referral, or check in the classified sections of reptile oriented magazines for the reptile-qualified veterinarian closest to you.

Quarantine

To prevent the possible spread of diseases and parasites between day geckos, it is important that you quarantine new specimens for a given period of time. A week would be the minimum time, a month is much better. During this time each quarantined gecko should be in a cage by itself, and you should be carefully sterilizing your hands and any equipment you may use between cages. During quarantine, take the time just to watch your lizard. Fecal exams should be carried out to determine whether or not endoparasites are present. For this, you simply take a fresh stool sample to your reptile veterinarian. The quarantine area should be completely removed from the area in which other reptiles are kept, preferably in another room.

The quarantine tank(s) should be thoroughly cleaned and sterilized prior to the introduction of the new lizard(s), and should be regularly cleaned throughout the quarantine period. As with any other terrarium, the quarantine tank should be geared to the needs of the specimen it is to house. Temperature, humidity, size, lighting, and all other factors must be considered.

Only after you are completely satisfied that your new specimen(s) is(are) healthy and habituated should it/they be brought near other specimens.

Respiratory Ailments

Day geckos are not particularly prone to respiratory ailments of any kind, but should one occur it can quickly debilitate a choice specimen. Respiratory ailments can be caused by overly damp and cold shipping or caging conditions, or other kinds of improper husbandry. Respiratory ailments can be of viral or bacterial origin and will require

The blotchy color of the yellow-throated day gecko, *P. flavigularis*, indicates stress.

nasal or mucal swabs to determine the sensitivity of the causative agents to a particular medication. A day gecko suffering from a respiratory problem may display labored breathing through a partially opened mouth. While awaiting a medical opinion elevate and maintain the cage temperature at 85–90°F around the clock.

Mouth Rot

Infectious stomatitis is another malady that is seldom seen in day geckos. It is caused by bruising of the snout and mouth. The infection will cause the soft tissue to be puffy, soft, and discolored, and a cheesy exudate may be present between the teeth. If untreated this can cause jawbone deterioration, tooth loss, and eventual death. Topical Neosporin and/or sulfa drugs are the medications of choice, but if a positive response is not quickly seen, consult your veterinarian.

Torn Skin

The skin of a day gecko is both beautiful and delicate. Small bruises and tears can be caused by males sparring, but huge tears can be caused by improper caging or handling. Two male day geckos should not be housed together. The bruises and small tears will heal and may become almost invisible after a few sheds. Large tears may need an application of Liquid Skin and/or veterinary intervention.

Broken Tail

Day geckos autotomize their tail with remarkable ease. Although temporarily disfiguring, tail loss is a natural method of escaping predators. It does not threaten the animal's health and tail regeneration is rapid and quite complete.

Metabolic Bone Disease

Day geckos are especially prone to MBD. This is an insidious disease that is caused by improper nutrition, specifically by too little dietary calcium or, if calcium is present in suitable amounts, by the inability of the lizard to metabolize it properly. The role of ultraviolet light, vitamin D3, and calcium is discussed in detail in the caging section on page 30. MBD is characterized by pliable bones, swollen legs, and a foreshortened or puffy look to the face.

Stress

Day geckos kept too cool, too crowded, too hot, or subjected to aggression by dominant terrarium mates will display certain signs of stress. Among these are a tendency for the subordinate specimen(s) to continually hide, to feed poorly or not at all, to be contantly fearful and nervous, and to persistently display an abnormal coloration (usually dark). Stress can prove fatal to an otherwise healthy gecko. Observe your day geckos frequently and get to know what are, for yours, normal colors and responses. Certain species are more aggressive toward tankmates than others; check the individual species accounts for details. Stress may be reduced by adding visual barriers, by placing your animals in a larger cage, by adjusting cage temperature, or by adding additional females. If stress continues after all of these corrective

measures, you will have no choice but to separate your specimens into individual terraria. If this becomes necessary, it is usually possible to periodically (and temporarily) move the male to the female's container for the purpose of breeding. Watch carefully for signs of overt aggressiveness toward the female by the male. It may be necessary to again separate the two almost immediately. If they are relatively compatible it still may be necessary to again separate the two after breeding has been accomplished. Observe and be ready to take whatever steps are necessary.

Skin Shedding

All lizards shed their skin. Shedding occurs with more frequency during periods of fast growth or to repair skin damage. Shedding results from thyroid activity. As the old keratinous layer loosens from the new one forming beneath it, your day gecko may take on an overall grayish or silvery sheen. When shedding has been completed your specimen will again be as brightly marked as it was to begin with.

The very dull coloration of this peacock day gecko discloses that this lizard is badly stressed.

As demonstrated by this gold-dust day gecko, when shedding, the skin is grasped in the jaws, pulled free, and eaten.

Although it seems that wild geckos seldom have problems shedding, some captives may. Shedding problems may often be associated with newly imported specimens, specimens that are dehydrated or in otherwise suboptimal condition, or when the relative humidity in the gecko terrarium/cage is too low. Shedding problems are most often associated with toes and tail tips. Day geckos are adept at removing these problematic pieces themselves, but if they do not succeed, then their keeper must intervene very carefully. Leaving dried skin in place can result in toe or tail tip loss. If patches of skin adhere, a gentle misting with tepid water or a daub of mineral oil from a cotton swab may help make removal easier.

Skin infections are not common, but may occur if a day gecko's terrarium is too humid. Check the preferred habitat of your gecko in the chart (pages 18–19) and alter your terrarium's humidity accordingly.

Broken limbs and other physical injuries can occur if your day gecko is dropped, if it falls, or even if it jumps from a moderate height. These injuries can also happen if the gecko is trapped beneath or in back of a shifting piece of heavy cage furniture.

If severe enough to be at all debilitating, veterinary assessment should be sought immediately.

Parasites

Although day geckos do not seem plagued by endoparasites, some may have harbor these pests. Endoparasites may cause bloody stools or other intestinal discomfort. Because of the complexities of identifying endoparasites and the necessity of accurately weighing specimens to be treated and measure purge dosages, eradicating internal parasites is best left to a qualified reptile veterinarian. It is important to use the correct medications and correct dosages. Because of the small size of the patient, there is no room for error.

The Language of Color

When discussing color in day geckos, we do not yet have any designer colors—albinos, leucistics, melanistics, or other aberrancies—to discuss and document. There are, however, many subtle variations of normal colors seen in

Large-blotched lined day geckos often have very blue tails.

Note the blue-edged black spot posterior to the arm of this peacock day gecko.

these lizards. Some variations are normal; some are otherwise induced.

When healthy, happy, and content (nonstressed) most day geckos are brightly hued in Kelly greens, blue-greens, or intense reddishbrowns. A few are clad in scales of gray or olive-tan. Although when inactive a few (*P. sundbergi*, for example) may assume a very dark coloration, color changes are more often indicative of stress or illness. Is the color change short-lived or does it persist?

Stress and illness are both discussed in the section on day gecko health, but we will make mention of a few causes and solutions here.

Improper caging conditions (lighting, temperature, fright, nutrition, overcrowding, improper sex ratios in a single cage, and unsuitable hierarchies, among others) can cause both stress and illness. The cure, of course, is to rectify the cause(s).

Check the obvious first. Is your cage lighting bright enough? Is cage temperature suitable (82–88°F)? Is there something about the cage or its positioning that causes the gecko to be frightened? Is the diet suitable and the vitamin-mineral intake proper and usable by the lizard(s)? Do you have too many day geckos housed in too small a cage or in a cage with insufficient visual barriers? Did you goof and place two males in the same cage? (If so separate them immediately.) Watch your gecko carefully for a sign of illness.

No day gecko is always at its brightest color. This would be as unnatural as having its color continually subdued. To be at its best your gecko needs to be contented. To determine that the conditions it needs to be so are adequate, you must learn gecko body language. Learning this is not difficult to do.

Breeding

One of the greatest thrills and challenges for those of us who maintain reptiles is finding and utilizing the keys necessary to breed them successfully. Fortunately, most day geckos respond well to captive conditions, and once settled in, most do not hesitate to breed. It is not difficult for a herpetoculturist to meet and exceed minimum criteria needed to have day geckos reproduce.

The criteria are simple: provide an adequate diet with ample vitamin and mineral additives, provide suitable caging (including space, temperature, lighting, and security, and egg-deposition sites), and be sure both sexes of day geckos are present.

It may take day geckos a few weeks to a few months to settle into a new cage and to adapt to a new regimen of care. However, once they have become accustomed to their surroundings and staked out their territories, breeding may occur frequently, and for many months of the year.

Female day geckos have a mineral storehouse—an endolymphatic (or chalk) sac at each side of the throat. It is thought that the calcium stored here is used in eggshell development. With some species, such as Standing's and giant day geckos, these sacs are prominent. They are less so on other species.

Females of most species of day geckos have insignificant femoral and preanal pores, whereas those of the males are obvious and large. The comparative size of these pores (openings in the femoral and preanal scales) is the best way of determining your gecko's sex.

The mid-body heaviness of this neon day gecko is caused by developing eggs.

Note the calcium-containing endolymphatic sacs on the throat of this female Standing's day gecko.

Depending on the species, day geckos may deposit their clutches in one of two ways. Some are "egg gluers." The pliant eggs of the gluers are placed by the female on a plant leaf or other piece of cage furniture, or the lizard may choose a side panel or corner of her terrarium on which to glue the eggs. Once the shells of the eggs have dried, the eggs can not safely be removed from the surface on which the female placed them. Although a leaf or a small piece of cage furniture may be removed from the terrarium and placed in an incubator, you will need to be more ingenious to successfully incubate eggs on the terrarium side. But it is possible to do so. You just need to assure that the eggs are given proper humidity and a temperature from 78 to 86°F (80–84°F is better). An easy way of incubating glued eggs is to tape a small plastic cup containing a small amount of moistened (and moisture retaining) material such as sphagnum moss or a paper towel over the eggs. To avoid mold growth, care must be taken that neither the cup nor the moisture-containing medium is in contact with the eggs. A few pinholes in the bottom of the plastic container will facilitate a slight air exchange (assuring that the developing embryos are not deprived) but not seriously deplete the needed humidity retention. It may be necessary to remove the cup and remoisten the medium periodically.

This female neon day gecko is rolling her eggs to dry the shells.

Once the shells of the eggs of the nongluers have hardened, those eggs may be removed from their deposition site and placed in the incubator. Again, a temperature from 78 to 86°F (80–84°F is best) and a high humidity are needed.

Incubating Day Gecko Eggs

We suggest an incubation medium of either fine vermiculite or sphagnum moss. This must be moistened to a proper consistency and kept at a suitable temperature. We use an inexact but simple way of determining the proper moisture content of the incu-bation medium. Moisten it thoroughly, then squeeze it as dry as possible in your tightened fists. Place a small piece of rigid plastic (a piece cut from the lid of a margarine tub, or similar container, or the ridged top of a film canister is fine) atop the moistened medium and place the eggs atop the plastic. The idea is to provide constant humidity but to prevent the eggs from actually coming in contact with the moistened medium.

Depending on the species of your geckos and the temperature at which the eggs are incubated, the incubation duration will usually be between six and twelve weeks. Plan to have food on hand (tiny insects such as hatchling crickets or the

Hatchlings of the Madagascar giant day gecko, *P. madagascariensis grandis*, are also strongly patterned.

Developing eggs can be clearly seen through the belly wall, as can calcium-bearing endolymphatic sacs through the throat, of this neon day gecko, *P. klemmeri.*

Hatchlings of Seipp's day gecko, *P. seippi*, are almost translucent.

fruit-honey mixture) when the geckos emerge.

Besides the duration of incubation, the sex of your hatchling gecko will be determined by the incubation temperature. Day geckos are among the many reptiles known to have their sex determined by the temperature at which the eggs are incubated rather than by genetics. This is called temperature-dependent sex determination and abbreviated TDSD. Varying temperatures (77 to 85°F) will usually produce geckos of both sexes. Eggs incubated at the warmer end of the temperature range usually produce males, those at the cooler end, females.

Like most day geckos, *P. astriata,* has an interesting facial pattern.

The Comoro day gecko, *P. comorensis,* is not as intensely green as many species.

Making Your Own Incubator

Materials needed for one incubator:

1 wafer thermostat/heater (obtainable from feed stores; commonly used in incubators for chicks)

1 thermometer

1 Styrofoam cooler—one with thick sides (a fish-shipping box is ideal)

1 heat tape or hanging heating coil

1 electrical cord and wall plug

1 heavy wire shelf to hold egg containers an inch or two above the coiled heat tape

Your goal is to wire the thermostat between the heat tape and the electrical cord, in order to regulate the amount of heat produced by the heat tape.

Cut the electrical cord off the heat tape, leaving about 18 inches of the cord on the heat tape. Make a hole through the side of the styro box, about 5 inches below the top edge. Pull the electrical cord through the hole, leaving the plug end outside (don't plug it in just yet!). Strip off about a half-inch of the insulation from the wiring at the cut end, and separate the two wires for a few inches.

Coil the heat tape loosely in the bottom of the Styrofoam box, making sure that it doesn't cross over itself at any point. Coil the tape so the recently cut end is near the electrical cord. Strip off about a half-inch of the insulation from the end of the wiring, and separate the two wires for a few inches.

Using one of the wire nuts, connect one of the red wires of the thermostat to one of the electrical wires of the heat tape. Use a second nut to connect the second red wire of the thermostat to one of the wires of the electrical cord. The third nut is used to connect the second wire of the electrical cord to the second wire of the heat tape (in effect, reestablishing part of the original wiring between the heat tape and its electrical cord.)

That's all there is to it. Put the lid on the cooler, and plug in the thermostat/heater. Wait half an hour and check the temperature.

The L-shaped pin on the top of the thermostat is the rheostat; turn it to increase or decrease the temperature inside your new incubator. You want the inside to be 80–86°F (27–30°C).

Once you have the temperature regulated, add your hardware cloth "shelf," and put the container of eggs atop the shelf. Close the egg container.

Day gecko eggs are calcareous. Some species attach their eggs to plants or other solid materials; some don't. If the day gecko eggs are attached to a plant leaf, leave the eggs on the leaf as positioned, snip that part of the leaf off, lay it on top of a plastic jar lid (or other such material), and lay the lid on top of the hatching medium. If the eggs are loose in the terrarium, remove them carefully (trying to retain the position in which they are lying) from the terrarium and place them on a small piece of flat plastic on the medium.

Check the temperature daily and add a little water to the incubating medium as needed. The preferred humidity is 80–90 percent. A saturated atmosphere in which the moisture condenses and drips onto the eggs is not wanted. The medium of vermiculite or perlite should be damp to the touch but too dry to release any water when squeezed by your hand. Do not wet the eggs when you are remoistening the medium.

Unlike the soft-shelled eggs of the leopard and fat-tailed geckos, it is difficult to ascertain fertility of the hard-shelled eggs of day geckos. Infertile eggs may discolor but will not collapse. If you are certain the eggs are infertile, they may be removed and discarded. For any number of reasons, embryo death may occur during incubation, or even as the full-term young are trying to break from their eggs.

At the end of the incubation period—which may vary in duration from about forty to more than eighty days—the baby day geckos will pip.

The babies may remain in the pipped egg for several hours, or may emerge almost immediately. Once they have hatched they should be moved to another terrarium and offered food, a sunning spot, and water. Their postnatal shed should take from several hours to a few days.

Glossary

Ambient temperature: The temperature of the surrounding environment.

Arboreal: Tree-dwelling.

Autotomize: The ability to break easily or voluntarily cast off (and usually to regenerate) a part of the body. This is used with tail breakage in lizards.

Brille: The transparent eye cap or spectacle that covers the eyes of a day gecko.

Caudal: Pertaining to the tail.

Cloaca: The common chamber into which digestive, urinary, and reproductive systems empty and which itself opens exteriorly through the vent or anus.

Congeners: Species in the same genus.

Deposition: As used here, the laying of the eggs.

Deposition site: The spot chosen by the female to lay her eggs.

Dorsal: Pertaining to the back; upper surface.

Dorsolateral: Pertaining to the upper sides.

Dorsum: The upper surface.

Endolymphatic sacs: A pair of calcium-containing organs beneath the chin of female day geckos.

Gravid: The reptilian equivalent of mammalian pregnancy.

Juvenile: A young or immature specimen.

Lamellae: The transverse scales that extend across the underside of a gecko's toes.

Lateral: Pertaining to the side.

Middorsal: Pertaining to the middle of the back.

Midventral: Pertaining to the center of the belly or abdomen.

Ontogenetic: Age-related changes.

Oviparous: Reproducing by means of eggs that hatch after laying.

Posterior: Toward the rear.

Subdigital: Beneath the toes.

Taxon: A species (taxa is the plural).

Thermoregulate: To regulate (body) temperature by choosing a warmer or cooler environment.

Vent: The external opening of the cloaca; the anus.

Venter: The underside of a creature; the belly.

Ventral: Pertaining to the undersurface or belly.

Ventrolateral: Pertaining to the sides of the venter (belly).

Note: Other scientific definitions are contained in the following two volumes:

Peters, James A. 1964. *Dictionary of Herpetology.* New York: Hafner Publishing Co.

Wareham, David C. 1993. *The Reptile and Amphibian Keeper's Dictionary.* London: Blandford.

Helpful Information

Herpetological Societies

Reptile and amphibian groups exist in the form of clubs, monthly magazines, and professional societies, in addition to the herp expos and other commercial functions mentioned elsewhere.

Herpetological societies (or clubs) exist in major cities in North America, Europe, and other areas of the world. Most have monthly meetings, some publish newsletters, and many hold or sponsor field trips, picnics, or indulge in various other interactive functions. Among the members are enthusiasts of varying expertise. Information about these clubs can often be learned by querying pet shop employees, high school science teachers, university biology department professors, or curators or employees at the department of herpetology at local museums and zoos. All such clubs welcome inquiries and new members.

Two of the professional herpetological societies are

Society for the Study of Amphibians
  and Reptiles (SSAR)
Dept. of Zoology
Miami University
Oxford OH 45056
http://www.muohio.edu/~SSAR

Herpetologist's League
c/o Texas National Heritage Program
Texas Parks and Wildlife Dept.
4200 Smith School Road
Austin, TX 78744

The SSAR publishes two quarterly journals: *Herpetological Review* contains husbandry, range extensions, news of ongoing field studies, and so on, whereas the *Journal of Herpetology* contains articles more oriented toward academic herpetology.

Hobbyist magazines that publish articles on all aspects of herpetology and herpetoculture (including lizards) are

Reptiles
P.O. Box 6050
Mission Viejo, CA 92690
*http://www.animalnetwork.com/
  reptiles/default.asp*

Reptile and Amphibian Hobbyist
Third and Union Aves.
Neptune City, NJ 07753
http://www.TFH.com

The hobbyist magazines also carry classified ads and news about herp expos.

The classified ads on *www. kingsnake.com* are a wonderful resource for geckos and other herps, and *PetPlace.com* is a good source of general information about many species.

Index

Breeding, 38–43
  Egg disposition, 39
  Egg incubation, 40, 42–43
  Sexing, 38
Caging, 25–30
  Furniture, 25–29
  Lighting, 30
  Plantings, 25, 29, 30
  Space requirements, 25
Choosing, 15, 24
Day Geckos
  Abbott's, 19, 23
  Agalega, 18
  Andaman Islands, 18
  Anjouan Island, 12
  Barbour's, 2, 18
  Black-lined, 19
  Blue-tailed, 5, 18
  Boehme's, 5, 6
  Boettger's, 18
  Comoro, 12, 16, 18, 20, 21, 41
  Drab, 19
  Dull, 13, 14, 18
  Dwarf, 19
  Flat-tailed, 9, 10, 12, 19
  Gold-dust, 7, 19, 27, 36
    Northwestern, 9
  Grand Comoro, 10, 12
  Koch's, 5, 6, 28
  Lined, 2, 12, 13, 18, 20, 37
    Northern, 19
    Southern, 18
  Madagascar, 5, 10, 28, 40
    Day, 4
    Giant Day, 4, 19

Mauritius forest, 41
  Merten's, 19
  Modest, 18
  Moheli Island, 11, 12
  Muted, 12
  Neon, 3, 11, 13, 19, 20, 38, 39, 40
  Northwestern, 18
  Ornate, 14, 17, 19, 30
  Pasteur's, 11, 12
  Peacock, 8, 10, 19, 24, 26, 29, 35, 37
    Two-spotted, 18
  Pemba Island, 18
  Reunion, 18, 21
  Rodrigues, 18
    Giant, 18
  Round Island, 18
  Seipp's, 10, 11, 12, 19, 41
  Seychelles, 19, 20
    Giant, 4, 7
  Spotted, 12, 14, 19
  Standing's, 3, 4, 6, 7, 17, 19, 26, 28, 39
  Three-lined, 18
  Yellow-throated, 8, 10, 12, 19, 34
Diet, 3, 31–32
  Calcium, 31
  Fruit-honey mixture, 3, 31
  Insects, 3, 31
  Vitamin D3
Endolymphatic sac, 38
Health, 33–37
  Broken limbs, 31
  Broken tail, 16, 20, 34

Metabolic bone disease, 34
Mouth rot, 34
Parasites, 36
Quarantine, 33
Respiratory ailments, 33
Rubberleg, 2
Skin shedding, 35, 36
Skin infections, 36
Stress, 35, 36, 37
Temperature, 37, 39
Torn skin, 16, 34
Heirarchies, 28
Obtaining, 20
  Payment, 22
  Shipping, 22
  Sources, 24–28
Phelsuma, 2
  abbotti ssp., 19, 23
  andamanensis, 18
  astriata ssp., 19, 41
  barbouri, 18
  beufotakensis, 18
  bimaculata, 18
  borbonica ssp., 18
  breviceps, 18
  cepediana, 5, 7, 18
  comorensis, 12, 18, 41
  dubia, 13, 14, 18
  edwardnewtoni, 2, 18
  flavigularis, 8, 10, 19, 34
  gigas, 2, 14
  guentheri, 14, 18
  guimbeaui ssp., 18
  guttata, 12, 14, 19

klemmeri, 4, 13, 19, 40
  laticauda, 8, 9
    angularis, 3
    laticauda, 7
  leiogaster ssp., 16, 18
  lineata ssp., 12, 19
  madagascariensis, 19
    boehmei, 6
    grandis, 4, 40
    kochi, 6, 28
    madagascariensis, 4, 5, 18
  minuthi, 18
  modesta, 18
  mutabilis, 12, 14, 39
  nigristriata, 19
  ornata, 14, 19, 34
    ornata inexpectata ssp., 21
  parkeri, 18
  pusilla, 19
  quadriocellata ssp., 8, 9, 19
  robertmertensi, 19
  trilineata
    seippi, 10, 11, 19, 41
  serraticauda, 9, 10, 11, 19
  standingi, 3, 7, 19
  sundbergi, 19, 37
    sundbergi ssp., 7, 19
  v-nigra, 12, 18
    anjouanensis comoraegrandensis, 12
    pasteuri, 11, 12
    v-nigra, 11, 12
Sex determination, 41